BACKYARD WILDLIFE

Geese

By Megan Borgert-Spaniol

BLASTOFF!
READERS

Note to Librarians, Teachers, and Parents:

Blastoff! Readers are carefully developed by literacy experts and combine standards-based content with developmentally appropriate text.

Level 1 provides the most support through repetition of high-frequency words, light text, predictable sentence patterns, and strong visual support.

Level 2 offers early readers a bit more challenge through varied simple sentences, increased text load, and less repetition of high-frequency words.

Level 3 advances early-fluent readers toward fluency through increased text and concept load, less reliance on visuals, longer sentences, and more literary language.

Level 4 builds reading stamina by providing more text per page, increased use of punctuation, greater variation in sentence patterns, and increasingly challenging vocabulary.

Level 5 encourages children to move from "learning to read" to "reading to learn" by providing even more text, varied writing styles, and less familiar topics.

Whichever book is right for your reader, Blastoff! Readers are the perfect books to build confidence and encourage a love of reading that will last a lifetime!

This edition first published in 2012 by Bellwether Media, Inc.

No part of this publication may be reproduced in whole or in part without written permission of the publisher. For information regarding permission, write to Bellwether Media, Inc., Attention: Permissions Department, 5357 Penn Avenue South, Minneapolis, MN 55419.

Library of Congress Cataloging-in-Publication Data
Borgert-Spaniol, Megan, 1989-
Geese / by Megan Borgert-Spaniol.
   p. cm. – (Blastoff! readers. backyard wildlife)
Includes bibliographical references and index.
Summary: "Developed by literacy experts for students in kindergarten through grade three, this book introduces geese to young readers through leveled text and related photos"–Provided by publisher.
ISBN 978-1-60014-722-7 (hardcover : alk. paper)
1. Geese–Juvenile literature. I. Title.
QL696.A52B677 2012
598.4'17–dc23   2011029088

Printed in the United States of America, North Mankato, MN.

010112   1207

Contents

Geese are birds
with long necks
and large wings.

They live near ponds, rivers, and **marshes**. They use their **webbed feet** to swim.

Geese eat berries, grasses, and seeds. Their **bills** have sharp edges that help cut their food.

Geese also eat **aquatic** plants. They tip upside down to find food underwater.

Most geese **migrate** to warmer areas in the winter. They travel in **flocks**.

Flocks fly in the shape of a "V." The geese talk to each other with loud honks.

Baby geese are
called goslings.
They have
soft feathers
called **down**.

Goslings can swim right away. They learn to fly when they are two months old.

Geese must protect their goslings. They flap their wings and hiss at **predators**. Stay away!

Glossary

aquatic—living in water; aquatic plants grow in water.

bills—the mouths of geese

down—soft feathers; goslings are covered in down.

flocks—groups of geese

marshes—wetlands with grasses and plants

migrate—to travel; most geese migrate south for the winter.

predators—animals that hunt other animals for food

webbed feet—feet with thin skin connecting the toes

To Learn More

AT THE LIBRARY

Bang, Molly. *Goose*. New York, N.Y.: Blue Sky Press, 1996.

Best, Cari. *Goose's Story*. New York, N.Y.: Farrar, Straus and Giroux, 2002.

Sayre, April Pulley. *Honk, Honk, Goose! Canada Geese Start a Family*. New York, N.Y.: Henry Holt, 2009.

ON THE WEB

Learning more about geese is as easy as 1, 2, 3.

1. Go to www.factsurfer.com.

2. Enter "geese" into the search box.

3. Click the "Surf" button and you will see a list of related Web sites.

With factsurfer.com, finding more information is just a click away.

Index

The images in this book are reproduced through the courtesy of: Dennis Donohue, front cover; Marty Ellis, p. 5; Dennis MacDonald / Alamy, p. 7 (top); Ellwood Eppard, pp. 7 (left, middle, & right), 9 (left & right); Johann Schumacher / Photolibrary, p. 9 (top); Imagebroker RF / Photolibrary, p. 11; Marie Read / naturepl.com, p. 13; Donald M. Jones / Minden Pictures, p. 15; Juniors Bildarchiv / Age Fotostock, p. 17; Robert McGouey / Photolibrary, p. 19; John Canalosi / Ardea, p. 21.